Talking Bronco

by the same author

★

ADAMASTOR

FLOWERING RIFLE

THE GEORGIAD

MITHRAIC EMBLEMS

BROKEN RECORD

FLOWERING REEDS

THE FLAMING TERRAPIN

THE WAYZGOOSE

TALKING BRONCO

by

ROY CAMPBELL

FABER & FABER LIMITED
24 Russell Square
London

*First published in Mcmxlvi
by Faber and Faber Limited
24 Russell Square London W.C. 1
Printed in Great Britain by
R. MacLehose and Company Limited
The University Press Glasgow*

Dedicated to
MARY CAMPBELL

Contents

One Transport Lost

Where, packed as tight as space can fit them
The soldiers retch, and snore, and stink,
It was no bunch of flowers that hit them
And woke them up, that night, to drink.

Dashing the bulkheads red with slaughter,
In the steep wash that swept the hold,
Men, corpses, kitbags, blood, and water,
Colliding and commingling rolled.

Some clung, like flies, in fear and wonder,
Clutched to the crossbeams, out of reach,
Till sprayed from thence by jets of thunder
That spouted rumbling from the breach.

In this new world of blast and suction,
The bulk-head tilted to a roof;
Friend aided friend—but to destruction,
And valour seemed its own reproof.

Forced by the pent explosive airs
In the huge death-gasp of its shell,
Or sucked, like Jonah, by their prayers
From forth that spiracle of Hell—

The ones that catapulted from it
Saw the whole hull reverse its dome,
Then ram the depths, like some huge comet,
Flood-lit with phosphorus and foam.

The shark and grampus might reprieve,
After their jaunt upon a raft,
The few that got Survivors' Leave—
But those who perished would have laughed!

Snapshot of Nairobi

With orange-peel the streets are strown
And pips, beyond computing,
On every shoulder save my own
That's fractured with saluting.

The Beveridge Plan

Through land and sea supreme
Without a rift or schism
Roll on the Wowser's dream—
Fascidemokshivism!

The Hoopoe

Amongst the crags of thyme and samphire,
The wastes of rosemary and fennel,
Up where the wolves in safety kennel
And by the gipsies' lonely campfire,
And round Toledo's shattered walls,
Where, like a crater in the moon,
The desecrated grandeur sprawls—
Though out of season, pitch, and tune,
All day the boding hoopoe calls.

The fire-bird flits amongst the cattle,
Pronouncing victory or doom,
The flashing corposant of battle,
The torch upon the hero's tomb,
The feathered tomahawk that waves
The bonnet of the redskin braves,
And cries once more his warning cry,
Before the grass has healed the graves
Or yet our open wounds be dry.

The comet of approaching war,
He flashes singing through the land,
And where his fiery crest is fanned
The farmyard poultry cluck no more.
Do cage-bred fowls resent this ranger
Of climes, who is the friend of danger
Yet visits, too, their sunless sky?
Is he not, too, a Southern Stranger
Whose gestures they would modify?—

But who has modified their own!
To have the lowdown from their cross-Fates,
Predicting tons of human phosphates
Imported here in flesh and bone,

In posh editions, for us mere
Shock-workers of the Camp and City
Whose sweat, and life-blood, is their beer.

Before me as the hoopoe cries,
I see a fiercer flag unrolled
Eclipsing now the red and gold
Infanta of the evening skies.
For now all other flags turn black
Save there, against the stormy rack,
Three crosses in a single wheel—
The spectrum of the light they lack,
And rainbow of the showers of steel!

But this no miracle-crusade
Won in our hearts before we strike;
Rather a punishment-parade
For friend and enemy alike;
Yet when the mealy mouths are heard
Of those who prostitute the word
And in the rearguard pimp for hire,
It's time to imitate the bird
Who preens his chevrons under fire!

To hear the Fire-bird change his score
And match his war-whoop to the drum
As scarce in twenty years before—
'Big Medicine' it was for some
Who with the hoopoe scoop the news
That is not printed in reviews—
The kind they stoned the prophets for,
And lumbering progress never views
Except to boycott or ignore.

This Bird be my heraldic crest
Because his prophecies are banned:

He chucks a regimental chest
And flits across the burning sand
To share those gifts of high bestowal
That seraphim bequeathed our sires
One winter night broadcasting 'Noel!'
(Strange news for Isidore and Joel)
To cattlemen by wayside fires.

Was that reported in 'The Prattler'
Or 'The New Yes-man' of those times,
Or like a diamond-headed rattler
Suppressed, along with Herod's crimes,
While he monopolised the Glaxo
And sopped his bib with granny's tears—
Though in a record flood for years
The baby-killing he attacks so
Had soaked him crimson to the ears!

To cock the wind this flame-red feather,
In my sombrero, be the sign
Prophetic of the coming weather
With no false hankering to 'fine',
And the diploma of a knowledge
So far beyond the scope of college
That whatsoever catch we croon,
Ages and continents, to acknowledge,
In blood or lava scrawl the rune.

1939

Dreaming Spires

Through villages of yelping tykes
With skulls on totem-poles, and wogs
Exclaiming at our motor bikes
With more amazement than their dogs:

Respiring fumes of pure phlogiston
On hardware broncos, half-machine,
With arteries pulsing to the piston
And hearts inducting gasolene:

Buckjumping over ruts and boulders,
The Centaurs of an age of steel,
Engrafted all save head and shoulders
Into the horsepower of the wheel—

We roared into the open country,
Scattering vultures, kites, and crows;
All Nature scolding our effrontery
In raucous agitation rose.

Zoology went raving stark
To meet us on the open track—
The whole riff-raff of Noah's Ark
With which the wilderness was black.

With kicks and whinnies, bucks and snorts,
Their circuses stampeded by:
A herd of wildebeest cavorts,
And somersaults against the sky:

Across the stripes of zebras sailing,
The eyesight rattles like a cane
That's rattled down an area-railing
Until it blurs upon the brain.

The lions flee with standing hackles,
Leaving their feast before they've dined:
Their funeral poultry flaps and cackles
To share the breeze they feel behind.

Both wart- and road-hog vie together,
As they and we, petarding smoke,
Belly to earth and hell for leather,
In fumes of dust and petrol choke.

We catch the madness they have caught,
Stand in the footrests, and guffaw—
Till shadowed by a looming thought
And visited with sudden awe,

We close our throttles, clench the curb,
And hush the rumble of our tyres,
Abashed and fearful to disturb
The City of the Dreaming Spires—

The City of Giraffes!—a People
Who live between the earth and skies,
Each in his lone religious steeple,
Keeping a light-house with his eyes:

Each his own stairway, tower, and stylite,
Ascending on his saintly way
Up rungs of gold into the twilight
And leafy ladders to the day:

Chimneys of silence! at whose summit,
Like storks, the daydreams love to nest;
The Earth, descending like a plummet
Into the oceans of unrest,

They can ignore—whose nearer neighbour
The sun is, with the stars and moon
That on their hides, with learned labour,
Tattooed the hieroglyphic rune.

Muezzins that from airy pylons
Peer out above the golden trees
Where the mimosas fleece the silence
Or slumber on the drone of bees:

Nought of this earth they see but flowers
Quilting a carpet to the sky
To where some pensive crony towers
Or Kilimanjaro takes the eye.

Their baser passions fast on greens
Where, never to intrude or push,
Their bodies live like submarines,
Far down beneath them, in the bush.

Around their heads the solar glories,
With their terrestrial sisters fly—
Rollers, and orioles, and lories,
And trogons of the evening sky.

Their bloodstream with a yeasty leaven
Exalts them to the stars above,
As we are raised, though not to heaven,
By drink—or when we fall in love.

By many a dismal crash and wreck
Our dreams are weaned of aviation,
But these have beaten (by a neck!)
The steepest laws of gravitation.

Some animals have all the luck,
Who hurl their breed in nature's throat—
Out of a gumtree by a buck,
Or escalator—by a goat!

When I have worked my ticket, pension,
And whatsoever I can bum,
To colonise the fourth dimension,
With my Beloved, I may come,

And buy a pair of stilts for both,
And hire a periscope for two,
To vegetate in towering sloth
Out here amongst these chosen few . . .

Or so my fancies seemed to sing
To see, across the gulf of years,
The soldiers of a reigning King
Confront those ghostly halberdiers.

But someone kicks his starter back:
Anachronism cocks its ears.
Like Beefeaters who've got the sack
With their own heads upon their spears;

Like Leftwing Poets at the hint
Of work, or danger, or the blitz,
Or when they catch the deadly glint
Of satire, swordplay of the wits,—

Into the dusk of leafy oceans
They fade away with phantom tread;
And changing gears, reversing notions,
The road to Moshi roars ahead.

The Skull in the Desert

to Desmond MacCarthy

I am not one his bread who peppers
With stars of nebulous illusion:
But learned with soldiers, mules, and lepers
As comrades of my education,
The Economy of desolation,
And Architecture of confusion.

On the bare sands where nothing else is
Save death, and like a lark in love,
Gyrating through the lift above,
The ace of all created things
Flies singing gloria in excelsis
And spreads the daybreak from his wings:

In an oasis of the Armour,
In a suspension of the thunder,
That, now relenting, seemed to sunder
A valley in the detonations,
And parted with a silken murmur
The mountainous reverberations:

Just where this solitude occurred
And like a rivulet was heard
The silence, dripping liquid verses,
Out of the smoke of burning cars,
The sulphurous methane of curses,
And orchestras of evil stars—

I found a horse's empty cranium,
Which the hyenas had despised,
Wherein the wind ventriloquised
And, fluting huskily afar,
Sang of the rose and the geranium,
And evenings lit with azahar.

22

Foaled by the apocalypse, and stranded,
Some wars, or plagues, or famines back,
To bleach beside the desert track,
He kept his hospitable rule,
A pillow for the roving bandit,
A signpost to the stricken mule:

A willing host, adeptly able,
Smoking a long cheroot of flame,
To catalyse the sniper's aim
Or entertain the poet's dream—
By turns a gunrest, or a table,
An inspiration, and a theme.

He served the desert for a Sphinx,
And to the wind for a guitar,
For in the harmony he drinks
To rinse his hollow casque of bone,
There hums a rhythm less his own
Than of the planet and the star.

So white a cenotaph to show
You did not have to be a banker
Or poet of the kind we know;
Subjected to a sterner law,
The brainless laughter of the ranker
Was sharked upon his lipless jaw.

No lion with a lady's face
Could better have become the spot,
Interrogating time and space
And making light of their replies,
As he endured the soldier's lot
Of dissolution, sand, and flies.

All round the snarled and windrowed sands
Expressed the scandal of the waves:
And in this orphan of the graves,
As in a conch, there seemed to roar
Reverberations of the Hand
That piles the wrecks along the shore.

If then I wished an understanding
Or could desire a synthesis,
It was with things of the abyss
Some way beneath our human standing
Of shearing, butchering, and branding—
Or bones anonymous as this.

Twice I had been the ocean's refuse
As now the flotsam of the sand,
Far worse at sea upon the land
Than ever in the drink before
For Triton, with his sons and nephews,
To gargle, and to puke ashore.

To look on him, my tongue could taste
The rigid mandibles of death
Between my cheeks. Across the waste
The drought was glaring like a gorgon,
But in that quaint, outlandish organ
With spectral whinny, whirled the breath—

The wind arrived, the gorgon-slayer,
Defied the dust that rose to whelm it,
And swirled like water in the helmet
Of that dead brain, with crystal voices
Articulating in a prayer
The love with which the rain rejoices.

24

The zephyr from the blue nevadas,
Stirruped with kestrels, smoothly rinking
The level wave where halcyons drowse,
Whirled with the hum of the cicadas,
With the green song of orchards drinking,
And orioles fluting in the boughs.

All the green juices of creation
And those with which our veins are red
Were mingled in his jubilation,
And hummed the swansong of the planet
Amongst the solitudes of granite
And the grey sands that swathe the dead.

All I had left of will or mind,
Which fire or fever had not charred,
Was but the shaving, rind, and shard:
But that sufficed to catch the air
And from the pentecostal wind
Conceive the whisper of a prayer.

And soon the prayer became a hymn
By feeding on itself. The skies
Were tracered by the seraphim
With arrows from the blue guitars
That on their strings funambulise
The tap-dance of the morning stars.

When frowsy proverbs lose their force
And tears have dried their queasy springs,
To hope and pray for crowns and wings
It follows as a thing of course,
When you've phrenologised the horse
That on the desert laughs and sings.

And we'll hand in our Ammo and Guns
As we handed them in once before,
And he'll lock them up safe; till our sons
Are conscripted for Freedom once more.
We can die for our faith by the million
And laugh at our bruises and scars,
But hush! for the Poet-Civilian
Is weeping, between the cigars.
Mellifluous, sweeter than Cadbury's,
The M.O.I. Nightingale (Hush!)
Is lining his pockets with Bradburies
So his feelings come out with a rush,
For our woes are the cash in his kitty
When his voice he so kindly devotes
In sentiment, pathos, and pity,
To bringing huge lumps to the throats
Of our widows, and sweethearts, and trollops,
Since it sells like hot cakes to the town
As he doles out the Goitre in dollops
And the public is gulping it down.
Oh well may he weep for the soldier,
Who weeps at a guinea a tear,
For although his invention gets mouldier,
It keeps him his job in the rear.
When my Mrs. the organ is wheeling
And my adenoids wheeze to the sky,
He will publish the hunger I'm feeling
And rake in his cheque with a sigh:
And when with a trayful of matches
And laces, you hawk in the street,
O comrades, in tatters and patches,
Rejoice! since we're in for a treat:
For when we have died in the gutter
To safeguard his income and state,
Be sure that the Poet will utter
Some beautiful thoughts on our Fate!

The Sentry's Reply to the Poet

The 'Sentry of your complicated heart'
Wishes you all the sympathies you carrot—
Soft sinecures: long wars: and space apart
To love humanity—and keep a parrot!

But here you cannot crash a bogus entry
Although the blitz was weathered by your Granny
Ere you came back to serenade the sentry,
Who thanks you with this bayonet in your fanny!

Here, till the pale aurora
Dismiss the stars from drill,
I dream of my Señora
Behind the guardroom grille.

In the outcry of the crickets
And the silence of guitars,
I watch the lonely pickets
And the slow patrol of stars.

Our vineyard and the terrace
By the Tagus, they recall,
With the Rose of the Sierras,
Whom I love the best of all!

My heart was once her campfire
And burned for her alone,
Fed with the thyme and samphire
That azure days had grown.

My thoughts for their safari
Have scarcely taken wings
Through spaces wide and starry
To hear her stroke the strings:

But ere one word be spoken
A Fiend my elbow jogs,
The reverie is broken
By the tomtom of the wogs:

And if I stage a fan-turn
My fancies singe and stink,
Like gnats around the lantern
That lights this cheerless clink.

And when my dreams grow flowery
They're put to panic flight
By an alcoholic 'shauri'
That preludes a drunken fight,

Till the curfew of the nighthawk
Cuts shrill into the tireless
And histrionic fight-talk
Of a wowser on the wireless:

And, all illusions killing,
Upon the stillness jars
A far hyaena drilling
His company of stars.

Washing Day

Amongst the rooftop chimneys where the breezes
Their dizzy choreography design,
Pyjamas, combinations, and chemises
Inflate themselves and dance upon the line.
Drilled by a loose disorder and abandon,
They belly and explode, revolve and swing,
As fearless of the precipice they stand on
As if there were religion in a string.
Annexing with their parachute invasion
The intimate behaviour of our life,
They argue, or embrace with kind persuasion,
And parody our dalliance or our strife.
We change ideas and moods like shirts or singlets,
Which, having shed, they rise to mock us still:
And the wind laughs and shakes her golden ringlets
To set them independent of our will.
They curtsey and collapse, revolve and billow—
A warning that, when least aware we lie,
The dreams are incubated in our pillow
That animate its chrysalis to fly.

The Clock in Spain

This Clock from England says he came
Where as a God he was revered.
His hours in length were all the same,
And each departed whence it came
The moment its relief appeared.

To a great Firm his line he traces,
Of manufacturers the aces,
And if you don't believe it's true,
The legend written on his face is
'Birmingham 1922'.

Squire was the Auden of those days
And Shanks the Spender of our trade;
For there the Clock awards the bays
And tells the prophets when to fade
Or die of one another's praise.

Like a policeman on his beat
The despot ticked with measured tread,
Dictating when to sleep, or eat,
Or drink—for in the darkest street
No Pub could open till he said.

Hours never telescoped in one
Disjointed by the lovers' thrill,
Nor made the night like water run
To strand the flushed and gasping sun,
Dumbfounded, on their window-sill.

Big Ben proclaimed, through mists of grime,
The surly fascism of Time,
And all the small Benitos, then,
Would cuckoo, tinkle, chirp, or chime
Their orders to the race of men.

35

Some Red Brigader, panic-shod,
Abandoned here, on Spanish sod,
This sacred fetish of his race
He'd fought to substitute for God—
So we took pity on his case:

And placed him on the mantel here,
Where still he ticked with might and main,
Though, like his countrymen, in vain,
With local ways to interfere
And stop the history of Spain.

The Sun would pause to hear a song
And loiter, when he chose to chime,
Which always put him in the wrong:
And folk would dance the whole night long
When he proclaimed it closing time.

His heart was broken by the trains
Which left him panting hours ahead:
And he was liable to sprains,
For on the wall we knocked his brains
Each time he shrilled us out of bed.

Like Bonaparte upon his isle
Confronted by Sir Hudson Lowe,
The Despot lost his haughty style
Recalling with a rueful dial
His pomp and pride of long ago.

But when, athwart an open door,
He smelt the orange-trees in flower,
And heard the headlong Tagus roar,
And saw the white sierras soar,
That moment cost him half an hour.

And when amidst the poplars white
He heard the nightingales unite
To drown the torrent's hoarse furore,
And held his breath from sheer delight—
It lost him fifty minutes more!

About the time of our Fiesta,
When gales from the meseta sweep
To strew the roses fetlock-deep—
He fell into his first siesta,
And now he often has a sleep.

But what served most to change his story
And turn his notions outside in—
This clock so querulous and hoary
Beheld my love, in all her glory,
Clearing for action to the skin:

Her hair that smokes with raven swirl
To tell of banked and hidden fire,
And golden dynamos that whirl
To launch a battleship of pearl
Into the rollers of desire.

He saw her deep dark eyes ignite
Like radium, or the northern light
That through the blackening ether flies,
And to the voltage of delight
In glittering swordplay fall and rise.

Her eyelashes with jet-black sting
Like scorpions curved: and dark as night
The chevrons on her brows that spring
Like feathers in a condor's wing
Arching their splendour in the height:

The ivory, the jet, the coral,
The dainty groove that dints her back
To take the sting from every moral
And made each jealousy or quarrel
The fiercer aphrodisiac.

The lips that burn like crimson chillies:
The valleys where the thyme uncloses:
The haunches like a bounding filly's:
Her breasts like bruised and bouncing roses—
And all the rest a field of lilies!

The room revolving like a wheel,
The romp, the tussle, then the fight,
The croup of galloping delight
Where rapture rides with rowelled heel,
Without a bridle, through the night.

Since then our clock has ceased to rail
Or tick the time, as if he knew
Time cannot change or custom stale
Those roses roaring in the gale
That, as I rode, around me blew.

Today more tractable you'll find him
And less on edge than was his wont.
In sprays of lilac we've enshrined him:
He stops the moment that you wind him,
Then starts up ticking, if you don't.

And now the pastures breathe their spice,
Twinkling with thyme and fresh anemone,
That punctuality's a vice
He swears today—and what a price
To have to pay for world-hegemony!

So silent with his rusty bell,
This ancient veteran of the shelf,
Whom I can neither pawn nor sell,
Reminds me somewhat of myself,
And if you want the reason, well,

Although he may appear to you
To have renounced his race and era,
His steel is British, cold, and blue,
As ever flashed at Waterloo
Or held the line at Talavera.

And if the dreadful hour should chime
For British blood, and steel as grim,
My clock will wake, and tick the time,
And slope his arms and march—and I'm
The one to fall in step with him.

The loud fire-eating propheteers
Will cross the drink in craven fears,
Or worse, like vulture, crow, and kite-hawk,
Engage in money-making fight-talk
And pick the bones of fusiliers.

Coining the opulence of Babbitts,
Out of the cowardice of rabbits
And mealy kisses of Iscariot,
More plutocratic in their habits,
The more they woo the proletariat—

In vain you'll ask of them the hour
When zero has begun to lower,
And that which pushed this idle pen
Will strike it forth in pride and power,
The trigger-finger on the Bren.

1939

After Rubén

One day an earthquake seemed to pass
I felt, with sudden dread,
As if a Babel made of glass
Were splintering in my head.

With Pascal's travelling abyss
I've toured: with Baudelaire
Have felt the wing of madness hiss
And graze my standing hair.

I know the insect in the ointment,
The weevil in the bread,
The eternal ache of disappointment
To all achievement wed.

But one must win at any price
And fight, to the last breath,
To be the Conqueror of Vice,
Of Madness, and of Death.

The Colloquy of the Sphinx and the Soldier

Across the sands and burning flints,
The huge Gibraltar of the Bints
With half a lion for her crupper,
She who defies the worm and weevil,
With sands and seas and stars coaeval,
Sits with eternity at supper;

Where not a shadow camouflages
The waters of the blue mirages
That sprout with sisal for their cress,
Confronting her, a soldier stands,
The flyblown Pharaoh of the sands
Whose pyramid's the Sergeants' Mess.

Conversing in the Esperanto
Of silence, whose majestic canto
The desert from the soul sublimes—
Of what they spoke I give the sense
Translated into mood and tense
But plead a licence for the rhymes.

'Rock-fortress of your sex and gender!
By "desert-ship" and donkey-tender
Elected as the Naval Base,
Where craft of shingly navigation
And caravans from half creation
Seek shelter from the howl of Space—

Can you assimilate the factors
Of planes, and carriers, tanks and tractors,
That threaten to subvert your reign,
Or from your fund of myth and story
Dispute, or parallel, the glory
Of England, at El Alamein?'

The Moon of Short Rations

Sound me the clash of eating-irons—
The wars where grease and gravy mix!
For in the wind I hear the sirens
Of convoys steaming up the Styx,
And here the rising moon enamels
The skulls of donkeys, mules, and camels,
Whose bonework trellises the track
From here to Headquarters and back,
Which vultures indicate by day
Who roost upon the cook-house shack
Too listless to be scared away.

In better lands, for men's relief,
The breeds for butchery are born,
And there the bullfrog booms his grief
Along the riversides of beef
At bullrise of the sacred horn,
The crescent, sickled in a trillion
Reflectors (Argentine, Brazilian,
Or African) through ranching lands,
Across the plains of bovril, bully,
And biltong, where the belt expands
And the warm air comes curled and woolly
With the refrain of bleating fleeces
Or bristly with the grunts of pork—
Moon of ineffable releases,
Clash me the clink of knife and fork!

Sing me of Sleeping-Car safaris
Through townships blown to smithereens:
The Gold-rush to the Manzanares
Of Bishops, Bards, and Picture-queens
With limelight free, and central heating,
Speeches, and healths, and fat men eating,

44

While children fought for stale sardines
The better to enhance their pity
And appetise the cocktail-snack,
And in the sewers of the city
We groped, and fought, and stumbled back.
Rivers of burgundy were roaring,
Burgundy that was blood of lives—
Poets, at Circe's shrine adoring,
Sound me the clash of forks and knives!

In better lands the green leaves mottle,
And Boreas opens out his throttle
Down speedways chevroned by the storks.
Lit by the red lamp of the bottle,
Flashes the play of knives and forks.
The Autumn comes with blare of snails
By shepherds blown with lungs of leather,
And where each huddled foothill quails
Beneath huge thundergrapes of weather,
The flocks descend to stockyard rails.
Great hides are stretching in the tannery,
The fat wind reeks with roasted beasts:
Gold in the twilight of the granary
Shimmer the nebulae of feasts.
And out of doors, behold, at morn,
The Samson tresses of the corn—
The strength of armies that expands,
And, vast as ocean, seems to spread
A blond Sahara, sown with hands,
Whose waves are blood, whose sands are bread.
There, when September winds were strident,
Amidst the sword-clash of the reeds,
We flew the sunrise on our trident
Above the groundswell of our steeds
That thundered into suds of spray,
Like some of those that Neptune breeds,

Nyanza Moonrise

Aurora to herself, whose white
Meridian, later, was my noon,
And then the dewed approach of night,
And then the rising of the moon.
That these four women were the same,
Though each was of the former born,
This moon reminds me now, whose flame
Bridges an absence as forlorn
Till, like her prayers, the far-shot rays,
Burnish my rifle, touch my brow,
And rule a pathway for my prow
Between the reefs and rocky bays,
With all Nyanza one round eye
To gaze her glory up the sky.

Reflections

While Echo pined into a shade,
Narcissus, by the water's shelf,
Met with a lurking death, and made
An alligator of himself.

Of many selves that meet in me
The meanest has the most persisted,
The one that joined the A.R.P.
When half humanity enlisted.

A shifty and insidious ghost,
Of all my selves he is the one,
Though it's with him I meet the most,
I'd go the longest way to shun.

When manhood crests the full red stream
Of comradeship, and breasts the surge,
Dreaming a chilled, amphibious dream,
He haunts the shallows by the verge.

Out of the mirrors in hotels
He makes for me, but as I pass,
Recedes into their glazing wells
And leaves no ripples on the glass.

Along the windows of the shops,
And in the tankard's curving base,
I have surprised him as he drops
Into the void without a trace.

He shaves the surfaces: he snails
His sheeny track along the walls:
The windows seem a myriad scales
Through which an endless serpent crawls.

His form is one, his number legion:
He incubates in hushed platoons,
Denizens of the glassy region
And of the vitreous lagoons.

Each time I step into the street
I multiply his gliding swarms,
Along the panes to launch a fleet
Of bloodless and reptilian forms.

I know the scar upon his cheek,
His limp, his stare, his friendly smile—
Though human in his main physique,
Yet saurian in his lurking guile.

Well on this side of make-believe,
Though edging always to the flanks,
He wears my chevrons on his sleeve
As though he'd earned them in the ranks

In him, behind each sheet of glaze,
A Eunuch with a bowstring hides:
Under each film, with lidless gaze,
A sleepless alligator slides.

Within his heart, so chilled and squamous,
He knows I've but to sell my pride
To make him safe, and rich, and famous;
And he would fatten if I died.

In feigned petition from the sash
He swerves to me, and I from him:
But if one day you hear a splash,
You'll know he's fastened on a limb.

No ripple on the glassy frame
Will show you where a man was drowned;
But Echo, practising his Fame,
Will pine once more into a sound.

Imitation (and Endorsement) of the Famous Sonnet of Bocage which he Wrote on Active Service Out East

Camoes, great Camoes! though twins in form
Tally the cursed fates that love to plague us,
Exchanging for our vineyards by the Tagus
The Sacrilegious Headland and the Storm:
Though, like yourself, from Chindwin to Zambezi
In wars and fearful penury I wander,
On vain desires my fevered sighs to squander,
And on the thorns of memory sleep uneasy:
Though trampled by the same vindictive doom,
I pray for sudden death to come tomorrow
And know that peace lies only in the tomb:
And though in shame and all precarious shifts
You were my model—mine's the crowning sorrow
To share your luck, but lack your towering gifts.

'Wars Bring Good Times for Poets'

(HEADLINE IN A DAILY PAPER)

Lies! Let the Leftwing Muse on carrion prey
To glut her sleek poltroons, the vulture's kin.
My only pickings were a ranker's pay,
With chevrons on my sleeve, and on my skin.

Jungle Eclogue

PERSONAE: Two British N.C.O.'s.   The Nat.

1ST N.C.O. It seems we've lost the way for good.

2ND N.C.O.   But, look!
  The hill has calved: and much, that we mistook
  For landscape, lives (unless it's my malaria)
  And moves, and grows, and profiteers in area.
  No random herd of buffalo or buck
  Could make the waking eyesight come unstuck,
  And from its focus swerve to such a pitch
  That bush, mirage, or vision—which is which?

1ST N.C.O. Now multiple, now single—yet I trace,
  Through all, the blurred refraction of a face;
  But if it has a voice that rumour seems
  Far less its own, than of the trees and streams,
  The whistling of a trillion leafy tongues
  To which the ancient forests heave their lungs.

2ND N.C.O. It scares me stiff. Let's slip into this wood
  And do a Spaunday while the going's good.

1ST N.C.O. This is some walking Hangover it seems
  Sent to molest us from the land of dreams,
  Or one of those old Fogies out of books
  That startle heroes with their gruesome looks,
  And of their birth and lineage make a song
  With genealogies four pages long,
  Men-mammoths of the Titan's hulking breed
  That late in history have run to seed,
  Or shifted off the road-maps and the charts
  To cultivate the Californian arts.

54

So showed the Polypheme to the companions
As here this weird abortion of the banyans:
So Caesar's country, bleeding from his sins,
With towers and castles for her curling-pins,
Took shape and met him at the swollen drift
Of Rubicon: so looming in the lift,
Shock-headed Adamastor, from his crag,
Came roaring down with sacrilegious brag
To scare the Lusiads, and (last March) ourselves,
Blaring his foghorn from the rocky shelves,
The day we slithered on the tilting deck
And half the convoy got it in the neck.
And so this Eye-sore to the Sergeants came,
MacCallion and MacNobody by name,
Though unlike others of his huffling race
He hesitates, it seems, to state his case.

2ND N.C.O. I fear some phoney mischief of the Japs
    To hypnotise us into booby-traps.
    I have him covered: shall I fire a burst?

1ST N.C.O. Our orders are—Diplomacy at first.
    Keep on the right side of the locals, aim
    To win their friendship and conserve the same.
    Who knows but this may be some playful Yogi
    Designing on our fears to come the Bogey?
    Elephantiasis, of Man, and beast,
    And spirit—is endemic to the east.
    Some outsize rustic yokel this may be,
    And harmlessly disposed to you and me:
    Some local Rhino-gelder, from his size,
    His odour, and the twinkle in his eyes,
    One who sustains the economic push
    De-lousing elephants from tracts of bush,
    Or some old-fashioned farrier of the thunder
    Who's fallen upon evil times (no wonder!) . . .

THE NAT. Wrong, every time! Your brains are both so slight
    That, even were they made of dynamite,
    They could not shift your forage-caps an inch.
    A Fleet of Bombers would not make me flinch—
    And so God help the first of you who plugs
    My Nat-ship with that squittering hose of slugs!
    In me you meet the father of the Nats
    But keep the knowledge underneath your hats
    Since no one will believe you if you don't,
    Or shoot a line according to your wont.
    Although my voice seems on the air to you,
    And you may think you've televised me too,
    And tele-stunk me—since you mention smells
    It's all in the derangement of your cells.
    Because your ears are singing with quinine
    Association falsifies the scene:
    You think in terms of Radio, as it hums,
    Fooled by squeak and whistle in your drums,
    And your disordered fancy does the rest
    Conjuring nightmares from your fevered breast:
    And so you clothe me in the forms you fear
    And in my voice—who knows but that you hear
    The fight-talk of some paunchy profiteer,
    Who broadcasts, dropping aitches for applause,
    And froths 'We workers' from his working jaws,
    Champing his red civilian hate to froth
    And tearing up his enemies like cloth,
    Though in his life he never did a stroke
    Save write best-sellers for the wealthy folk.
    You now insult me with his voice and tone
    And see, in me, the monster he has grown
    Since such as he can branch, a gruesome race,
    Their octopoid antennae through all space,
    Destructive Titans, greedy in the gripe,
    Long in the ears, and windy in the pipe,
    Drunk with their power, blaspheming as they strut,

And mischievous as monkeys on the rut;
These, through the waves of ether, towering rise
With gods and angels to dispute the skies,
Through waves of ether they can scold the stars
And scare the pale inhabitants of Mars
With toad-like hate puffed up beyond amaze
To rule your destinies and guide your ways,
Class against class, to their eternal loss,
To prime with hate—and all against the Cross;
And while they wolf the income and the cash,
To head your empire to its final crash.
As for 'free speech' for which you're bluffed to fight
It's theirs alone, to throttle as you write.
This is the breed you have entrenched at home
By volunteering (Fools!) to cross the foam.
Class them with Polyphemus, Adamastor,
And other bungling hawkers of disaster,
But I, the silent engineer of fate,
Despise that whole Canaille as out of date.
Such out-size hufflers of the beetling brow,
Beside me, are anachronisms now,
And he of whom you spoke, with Godless brag
Who shivers on the aviating crag
Above the rotary abyss, where three
Conflicting currents churn the polar sea—
Is but a quaint survival, whom you saw
Crunching a whole armada in his jaw.
Though, painted with the carnage of his quarrel
His sands were rubies and his foam were coral:
Though in his depths, sharked by the U-boat's crew,
The Red of British valour stripes the blue
As though to stain it yours, and with your blood
To colonise the whole rebellious flood:
Yes, though three Empires sank to stave his power,
There, where your Flag flutters its moth-like hour
And seems to you the iris of the battle

57

The solitude of coast-watches who've died
Of their own company—those hollow-eyed
Anchorites of the bush, through wounds or illness
Thrown out of fighting ranks, to face the stillness
Of jungle days. As when some ageing horse
Between the shafts has run his faithful course,
They sell him to the bullring; there he's torn
By the dread silence with its fearful horn
While fever claps the blinkers on his brain
And buries in his flank the spurs of pain;
He perishes with none to heed his call
Save some few scorpions in the crumbling wall.
Now, for your daft intrusion of my reign
You, too, must suffer penitence and pain,
But, for the fact that you have made me laugh,
I spare your next of kin the telegraph.
Prepare, then, to appreciate my art
As from these sacred precincts you depart.
First in the fleecy silence of the ward,
Where through the night I wave my ghostly sword,
Where the mosquito-nets like dangled spooks
Tower to the roof and curtsey on their hooks—
You will be wrung like linen of your sweat
And incubate the nightmares as you fret,
Till, at the tenth relapse, they'll fire you out
Unfit to soldier, but A.1 to tout.
Thence weak and stumbling with unsteady hand
Grope your way home—into a foreign land!—
To find that all you fought for (as you thought)
Has turned into the very thing you fought.
The self-same peoples that your oath defends
Against your foes: as if to make amends,
Now shriek beneath the talons of your friends,
Who trample treaties, cozen, and betray
And slaughter with the same delight as they,
Differing only in the fists or palms

That semaphore their imbecile salaams,
Except that, though it's stifled in the news,
Your friends hunt Christians as your foes the Jews
And seeing that the former are more numerous—
Why, that is what appeals to me as humorous!

1ST N.C.O. Arrest the bastard for despondent talk!

THE NAT. Come do your worst. The truth you cannot baulk:
I am within your blood, and all I've spoken
Is of your guttering morale the token.
And I can shake you worse, yes, clear your eyes
Until you envy those you most despise—
Him of the double seawake, in whose track,
Expelled by fear, by profit ogled back
Both ease and riches follow: him who sold
His country's youth for stolen Spanish gold
And pimping safely in the rear purveyed
Cheap bait for cannon fodder: him who prayed
For war, then farmed it in the M.O.I.,
Bewept poor soldiers that were doomed to die,
And beat the drum in loud heroic din
For a fat income and a scatheless skin:
The grigs and earwigs, safe beneath the boulder,
That you, poor Sisyphuses! stooped to shoulder,
And bending, sprained your backs for evermore.
These are the men for whom you won the war
Theirs is the freedom both of speech and thought
(Freedom to gag your own) for which you fought.
But for the Channel, and for such as you,
They would have been 'collaborators', too!
Then see your children head-lugged while you wait
From faith and family by the robot State,
Mass-hypnotised, dinned drunken by the tireless
Mechanic repetition of the wireless . . .

61

Who wish their abject souls unborn,
Subjected to their living radium
Returned, as athletes to the stadium,
Who'd come on creaking stretchers borne.

I did not come to dump my sins,
Which, stronger than a mule, I carried,
To their foul load so blithely married
They could not bring me to my shins
For any trick of thief or strumpet.
I came because I heard the Trumpet
When the mad victory begins!

So a loud ass, to be admired,
With no persuasion from the quirt
And heedless that his load is dirt,
By his own braying pibroch-fired,
Might leap the gate, and brave the scoffer,
And come his services to offer
Where snow-white chargers are required.

But from such eagle towers of pity
Eusebio heard my drab confession
That rumbled like a Red procession
When to the 'Meeting' roars the City
With lifted fist and lungs that bray,
His looks abashed that loud Committee
And sent them muttering on their way.

There, parted from those pistoleros,
I stood alone with what I am
As by a wrecked and burning tram.
The companies of drunken heroes
Whose valour varies with their numbers,
Dispersing, teetered to their slumbers,
And each as harmless as a lamb.

And though their fate I could resist,
That gallowed every workless wreck
To dangle from his lifted fist,
His arm a hangrope to his neck,
When like a clinical exhibit
The gesture of the Walking Gibbet
Has jerked him for the Jews to peck—

Yet, to be pitied from such height,
I felt what whets the frenzy-cursed
To slay these Witnesses the first,
Whose cold-and-hunger-bearing sprite,
To thrice their injuries resigned,
Reproaches and rebukes them worst
For so babooning from their kind:

Which, like a glass in a dark place,
Being so much in league with Light,
Might, glinting on the murderer's face,
Reveal him to his own affright,
Or, with a shimmer on the dirk,
Deflect it from the kind of work
That slinks, offended, from the sight.

Their Church, though poorer than an attic,
Anachronised, and seemed to void
Of meaning all that's Meetingoid,
Or tries to pass for Democratic—
More than the grievances they roar,
Its silence galled them to the core
That was so ageless and ecstatic!

But soon the Hoopoe, changing score,
The crested harbinger of battle,
That shares our life amongst the cattle
And only sings in times of war,
The corposant of coming slaughter,

Was singing by the blood-red water
As scarce in centuries before.

And Nature never lit that shore
Where ghost-white suns, foreboding, sank,
And, mirrored with our horses, drank
The flames of blood and liquid ore,
Where Tagus showed that Sky of skies
To which so many soon would rise,
With flames for feathers, streaming gore.

By every sign the times were known,
Humanity by day benighted,
The flesh defiled, dominion slighted,
Blasphemed the high, majestic throne,
And on each wind the whisper blown—
'The weak are strong in hate united,
Woe to the strong who ride alone!'

To those of Carmel half a stranger,
Their purchase from the farms I'd brought
With veld-flowers as an afterthought
That seemed too lovely for the manger,
And now, when ruin lit the towers,
Beset by death, and tracked with danger,
I could not break that chain of flowers:

But proudlier rode to their doomed door
Than ever, plumed and spurred, before
To thundering pigeon-flights of hands,
When, snowed with talc, cascading pearls,
And forested with jet-blue curls,
A whole Sierra made of girls
Sheers sunward from the bloodlit sands!

But Nero's Circus would have been as
A play, himself a paltry showman,

66

To this most awful of arenas
That stretched, Sahara to the Roman,
With half-a-million lives to spill,
Where to the howl of worse hyenas
I rode but as an alguazil.

The Carmelites, all terror quelled,
The first of the toreros came
In 'clothes of light' whose ghostly flame
Was only of the soul beheld,
To flaunt their crimson one by one:
And Death, in turn, by each was felled
Till valour seemed to fix the sun.

The Taurine Sun, in trancèd swoon,
Who loves to linger over peril
And late through evening skies of beryl
Will stretch a famous afternoon,
Had hung so long upon their valour
As, when the smoke dissolved in pallor,
To seem the chill, belated moon.

His radiant face when last I saw
Eusebio bade me take delight:
His flesh was flame, his blood its light
That sought the fire as fire the straw,
And of his agony so cruel
As ruthlessly devoured the spite
As eager flame devours the fuel.

Small wonder then as trash too earthy
The gunbutts drove me from the pin
They smashed to let such Princes in,
When, too presumptuous, as unworthy,
My carcase for a Crown to barter,
The blows acceding to the Martyr
Rebuffed me for a Harlequin.

67

In my black mask, with bleeding eyes,
I woke as one for gala dressed,
My scapular beneath my vest
Which only then I learned to prize,
And there, like Romeo, the mad lover,
In the forbidden town, discover
And hold the Loved-One to my breast.

So tenderly to fall enamoured
So late—Oh, what a fool was I
To blunder ignorantly by
Just when the third great Nail was hammered,
The strident spear had gashed the cry,
When dicers for the leavings clamoured,
And blood was streaming down the sky!

The Flood-rush, with their blood to break it,
Now filled the land with fire and slaughter.
The Tagus, that was running water,
Was now alive, if blood could make it
That had not had the time to die:
The town, if rushing flames could take it
Was half rebuilded in the sky—

As now a lunar landscape tells
With craters for its domes and spires,
The architecture of the shells,
The hollow sculpture of the fires,
Where memory, to grope its way,
Must seek in absence and dismay
The landmarks that it most admires.

But ages to this blackened tower
Will harness their momentous race
To find, like Tagus at its base,
A station of electric power

Whose Dynamo and sleepless mill
The Christian world with light may fill
And grind its life-sustaining flour:

Where faith-starved multitudes may quarry
As in a mountain, and be fed.
And well might Hell feel sick and sorry
To see the brown monks lying dead,
Where, as with coarse tarpaulins spread,
Each seemed a fifty-horsepower lorry
That to the troops had brought the Bread!

Their wounds were swords—how bravely worth
The care the angels took to smith them!
We thought they took their victory with them
But they had brought it down to earth,
For it was from their neighbouring spire
The proud Alcazar caught the fire
Which gave that splendour phoenix-birth.

A phoenix from its ash to father,
A greater, in its turn, to sire—
It was to be to the Alcazar
What the Alcazar is to Spain,
And Spain is to the world entire;
Unanimous in blood and fire
A single purpose lit the twain.

Like Etna and Vesuvius burning,
The reign of Sodom overturning,
We heard their coal-red lava roar,
While miracles reigned down like manna,
And from the hurricane furore,
An Eagle turned to a hosanna
That has not ceased to soar, and soar!

On the Martyrdom of F. Garcia Lorca

Not only did he lose his life
By shots assassinated:
But with a hatchet and a knife
Was after that—translated!

How it Works

Salute the free Utopian State
We fought for. Feed, but do not look.
For each free tuppence-worth of Bait,
They charge a dollar on the Hook!

En Una Noche Oscura

(Translated from St. John of the Cross)

Upon a gloomy night,
With all my cares to loving ardours flushed,
(Oh venture of delight!)
With nobody in sight
I went abroad when all the house was hushed.

In safety, in disguise,
In darkness, up the secret stair I crept,
(Oh happy enterprise!)
Concealed from other eyes
When all my home at length in silence slept.

Upon that lucky night,
In secrecy, inscrutable to sight,
I went without discerning
And with no other light
Except for that which in my heart was burning.

It lit and led me through,
More certain than the light of noonday clear,
To where One waited near
Whose presence well I knew,
There, where no other presence might appear.

O Night that was my guide!
O Darkness dearer than the morning's pride,
O Night that joined the lover
To the beloved bride
Transfiguring them each into the other!

Within my flowering breast,
Which only for himself entire I save,
He sank into his rest
And all my gifts I gave
Lulled by the airs with which the cedars wave.

Over the ramparts fanned,
While the fresh wind was fluttering his tresses,
With his serenest hand
My neck he wounded, and
Suspended every sense in its caresses.

Lost to myself I stayed,
My face upon my lover having laid
From all endeavour ceasing:
And, all my cares releasing,
Threw them amongst the lilies there to fade.

Monologue

No disillusionment can gravel,
A mercenary volunteer
Who joins an alien force, to travel
And fight, for fifty pounds a year.
A grizzled sergeant of the pommies,
A gaunt centurion of the wogs,
Can fall for no Utopian promise
The Bait of grasping demagogues.
Against the usurers of tears,
Fraternity, and all that dope,
I learned (while wet behind the ears)
The use of Nelson's telescope.
The Left Wing Prophet, Bard, and Seer,
Sleek Babbitts of the Age to Be,
Who farm this carnage from the rear
Have yet to find a fly on me.
I know the love that shears our fleeces,
The love that makes our thinkers fools,
The love of thirty silver pieces—
A soldier's value, or a mule's!
The same for all who trade in doves
And fatten on the world's distress,
The pedlars of fraternal loves,
And creeping Shylocks of the Press.
Against each rearguard propheteer
And Tartuffe from the M.O.I.,
Experience wads my dainty ear,
And through the solemn bluff, my eye,
For bayonet-practice, punching sawdust,
Lets in the glint I love to see—
For where the sacking gapes the broadest
The daylight laughs and winks at me!

I'm fighting for no better world
But for a worse—the blasted pit

73

Talking Bronco

In human history, and rightly so,
The Final Word is with the knockout blow,
Except when, to deride that mortal thud,
Courageous martyrs write it down in blood.
Were whacked malingerers to lay the rule
Of what we learn as history at school,
With 'Ifs' and 'Buts' to crutch their limping style
And maunder through the slow, pedestrian mile,
(And that's the role, on which I pulled the chain,
Our British Intellectuals played in Spain)—
We would learn suicide before our dates
And press precocious pistols to our pates,
For inquests than matriculations apter
Before we'd started on the second chapter.
Else, we prefer the company, in books,
Of smiling victors to disgruntled crooks,
When martyrs can't be found whose brighter crown
Outlasts the greenest laurels of renown.
So thus Spain had the verdict either way
Signed with her blood though she had lost the day,
Since five of her first leaders, that were six,
Rushed forth to seize a bridgehead on the Styx,
On duty killed, or that they scorned to fly
When for their blood was raised the wolfish cry:
A fluid Spain's Red 'leaders' never stop
To risk although they've promised 'the last drop'
Each time they led their bruisers (from the back)
To show a pair of heels to the attack,
Deserting both their wounded and their dead
For driven dupes, not free men bravely led.
As careful of their pockets as their skin
Except when their own comrades do them in
(As happened to Durruti and to Nin)
They left no redder stain their faith to write

Than what they sweat or piddled in their fright
In drops as yellow as their oaths were red—
And as they've written so shall they be read,
With all who try to stutter their apology
(From Duffduff down to Spaunday's last anthology)
And all who farmed the carnage for good pay
Though from the firing they kept far away.
For see the Pasionaria (with her swag)
Escaping weeks before they struck their flag,
Preceded by a dozen fat poltroons
Each with ten dewlaps frilled in red festoons
To pose for anticlerical cartoons,
And dice for loot, in Mexican saloons.
But when the golden guineas cease to clink
And some new racket heaves the seas of ink,
The truth will out, and cry from shore to shore
When Bloomsbury and Fleet Street are no more.
How stale would seem the Epic race of man
Seen through the blinkers of the Also-Ran!
So History looks the winner in the mouth
Though but a dark outsider from the South,
A Talking Bronco, sharked from ear to ear
With laughter, like a running bandolier,
With teeth, like bullets fastened in their clips,
To chew the thunder and to spit the pips,
Ejecting from the breech, in perfect time,
The shells of meter and the shucks of rhyme,
Yet drive the thoughts with perforating aim
Like tracer-bullets on their threads of flame.
Open my lid, inspect my Steinway grin,
And view the shining ivories within.
With such a gadget Samson quelled his foes
And rained the thundering mitraille of blows,
When he invented, chopping men like straw,
The first machine-gun from a Donkey's Jaw.
And shall I scorn such hardware, though my own,

77

Get posted to some rural Fireman's Pump,
To tend wet cabbages from catching fire
And guard the vicar cycling round the shire,
And advertise the fact on blurb and board
For public recognition and reward:
Or in the Admiralty, licking stamps,
To wear a uniform with golden clamps,
Out of his job some aged clerk to Jew
Who thrice as well as he the work could do—
Which Yesmann praises in his 'Emu Series'
(That Woolworthiser of ideas and theories)
Or at the most, if taken in the trawl,
Serve as a grudging Conscript if at all!
Deserters when devotion was most due,
But for the Channel and the bronco few,
They would have been 'Collaborators' too!

Then call me all the Horses that you like!—
You will not find such virtues in a Tyke
That follows beaten armies in the rear
Alternately beset with greed and fear
And brings bad luck to every cause he scabies
Far worse than if he'd bitten it with rabies.
No sooner his anthology came out
Than at the sign Spain had no further doubt:
Red hunted Red in carnage through the land—
And yet he blames us that we lent a hand!
His leash of heads will bark, as he has shown,
For every cause or country save his own
Fortunate Country! to avert an omen
Worse than the leftwing vulture to the Roman.
For where was he, when England stood alone?
This Bogus Proletarian, the Drone
Who stood beside the Worker (*while it paid*)
Seeks every ruse his Gospel to evade
Appeals to privilege of class and wealth,

80

To save his pockets and preserve his health,
In ministries, where cowardice makes free,
He settles, like the vulture on the tree,
Snuffling his snout in other people's gore
As first in Spain he learned the trick before
With his ten-guinea throat-lump, gilded tear,
And Fox and Metro bringing up the rear,
Commercialising slaughter, with the Deans,
Press-barons, Earls, Bishops, and Picture-Queens,
Who rushed headlong on Sleeping-car Safaris
And made their Klondyke of the Manzanares.
Where Briddish Intellectuals made their pile
And Book-Clubs flourished in prodigious style,
Survey the wilderness they made of Spain
As rich in Sobstuff as devoid of grain,
As fat with tragedy as lean of meat
And full of Copy as forlorn of wheat—
Since there's no villainy at which they'll rest
To cultivate the sobs that sell the best.
A more ferocious, bloodthirsty poltroon
Has never howled for blood beneath the moon
Than joint MacSpaunday, when his leash of heads
To murder, rape, and arson roared the Reds.
For then he 'stamped with emphasis' of tone
For 'Energy and Energy alone'.
He put the test to cruel, killing steel
And from his verdict there was no appeal!
But when in answer to his Fee-Fo-Fum
As to an urgent S.O.S. I come
With 'Death to Killers'—yes, he roared for that!—
And 'Energy' enough to knock him flat—
Before we've killed a fourth of what they've killed
Or half his rosy daydreams are fulfilled,
A greedy masochist for kicks and blows
He roars for 'Justice', as he feels it close,
And yells the more for it, the more he feels

It sink into his flanks with rising weals.
All Mealy-Mouthed, he changes now to ruth
And natters of 'Disinterested Truth'—
So poor Negrin when he'd destroyed the Church
And even the Devil left him in the lurch,
Turned to the Vatican his dying hope
And wired his sad condolence—for the Pope!
Yet what paid propaganda has to do
With abstract 'Truth' I'd rather not pursue—
Mine never was the nostrum-peddling manner
To wheedle you salvation—less a tanner.
And surely such Disinterest is funny
That's always on the side of Ready Money,
Nor further from the sales will swerve its spoor
Than ants from trickled honey on the floor,
With no more split between the heart and pocket
Than if the latter were a neckworn locket,
Always with the main chance to coincide
And never into danger glance aside.
Surely (it does not seem too much to plead)
Disinterestedness may sometimes lead
To other goals than those of fear and greed.
Nor does it always move with the same slouch
As the Full Belly and the Bulging Pouch,
Nor always keep so sleek and whole a skin
As wraps the Brave MacSpaunday snug within.
Sometimes at least its pathway may divide
And even with the Book-Trade may collide.
Sometimes its way from Fleet Street widely deviates
A craggy path, which no smug pub alleviates,
And if it's true it has its own set course
You have to hand it to the talking Horse
He sometimes shows that, when it pays the least,
He'll take the mountain path with winter fleeced,
Or volunteering, share the sand and heat
Without a leftwing carpet to his feet.

So if by your Disinterest you swear
Come, ask yourself MacSpaunday when and where
It ever swerved you by one tiny hair
From the main chance, or took a different route
From that which pure self-interest would suit.
Say to confront you with an angry mob
To get you boycotted, or lose your job,
Or land you here beside the talking Pony
Who can do other things than talk bolony.
Quote to me any phrase you ever uttered
Excepting on the side your bread was buttered,
And cite one single case when you were found
Save where the cash and comfort most abound,
As a fifth-column and a trojan horse
In Leftwing ranks to neutralise the force
Of Socialism; mixing milk and water
With the red vodka of diluvial slaughter,
Was it for such 'disinterested truth'
That you to butchers sold your country's youth,
Crazing them, like the Gadarene, to die
And trade their tender bacon for a lie,
While in the rear you fattened and grew cosy
By painting sham Utopias pink and rosy,
For which you'd never risk a scratch yourself,
But only brewed the dope for stolen pelf.
(The same, today, for E.L.A.S., you'd have dared
Had they a Gold Deposit to be shared.)
In vain might talking broncos counsel 'Slow!'
And all the direful consequences show
Exactly as it happened four years after—
It only raised some patronising laughter.
But oh, the consternation on your faces,
The day the Talking Bronco kicked the traces!
And though you'd howled for blood, and fire and arson,
Behold you now, the caterwauling parson,
A punctured Tartuffe, oozing mercy, ruth,

And justice, and 'disinterested truth!'
So off you went to call the wowsers' meeting
To ban the talking bronco from competing

The 'salted' horse that never need the vet see
Owes his inoculation to the tsetse:
Via the cobra's bite we get the serum,
And, further still, to illustrate my theorem,
Mythologers anticipated science
Applying homeopathy to giants;
The hydra is inherent to the hero:
In Fafnir's blood they douche the Herculero:
Achilles from the Styx his temper took,
With frothy gargle hissing in the brook,
Like a hot sword, whose handle was his heel,
Acquiring thus the properties of steel;
So I, in Lethe ducked a thousand times
By wishful critics, make a float of rhymes,
Deriving buoyancy from leaden spite
And like a pearly nautilus, or light
'Portuguese-man-of-war's' more airy kite,
Go sailing with a six-yard thread of sting—
And woe to him that mixes with the thing!

Free verse and prose are slippers for the dons
Unfit to clang this marching age of bronze:
The true vernacular a thorax throws
And leads the rhyme and meter by the nose;
It takes the gradients at a marching tread
Alert for all the ambushes ahead,
And when it finds some wild romantic dream
Has broken loose, with tousled hair astream,
It's easy to collect it on one's pen
As passing troops collect a wayside hen:
And many a dream poor Spaunday lives to cluck
Has ended thus, upon my bayonet stuck,

All neatly barbecued, with careless art,
To fritter on the campfire of my heart!
So you can back the couplet every time,
With its ten fingers twirling thumbs of rhyme,
To seize and clamp the trailing thoughts they fray
And scatter like tobacco by the way,
And in iambics fold them, nearly set,
As nimble fingers scroll a cigarette,
For memory to case them in his breast
And smoke at leisure, as it suits him best.
For what poor Spaunday never understands—
The couplet is a verbal pair of hands
With a two-handed punch, more clean and deft
Than his one-armed and butterfisted Left.
The stumps and bunions of our modern prose
And of free verse, will never pluck the rose,
Or lace the boot, or prime the hand-grenade
That sinks their pink Utopias in the shade,
Though flung from five years distance, in the dark,
To burst prophetic on the chosen mark.
I litter no parades with cornucopias
Of stale ice-cream, or derelict Utopias,
To lie like last week's picnic, spoil the view—
And leave one so much cleaning up to do!

My verse was nourished by Toledo's sun
In whose clear light Ray, Sword, and Pen are one,
One in her soldier-poets of the past,
And here again united in her last:
The Pen a sword, prophetic in advance,
Deriding probability or chance,
That with unerring skill and biting scorn
Can sack a dud republic ere it's born!
The sword a pen to chronicle its deed
And write in scarlet for the world to read:
And both the lightning's thunder-scribbled ray

To singe the daft illusions of the day.
So dazzlingly from hand to hand they switch,
No Leftwing Bard could tell you which is which:
Ere he can name the lightning, forked or sheet,
It whistles up his foothold from his feet,
And sprawls him headlong with its blinding beams
Amongst the wreck of moneymaking dreams.
Like three prongs of one trident, where one hits
The other two will finish off the bits,
Since all together in one flame unite
To foin, to flash, to thunder, or to write!

The libel law your fortified enclosure
To save you from debunking and exposure,
A hydra-headed monster you oppose
To my clean arms, an omnibus of foes,
Stuffed full to bursting like a cat with kittens
With a strange rout of Briddishers and Yitons,
And Bogus Freestaters, and guys gone Yank
Like some farced Trojan horse, or Bolshy tank
With its red farrow, sniping from its womb
At Christian Outposts: but I spell your doom
For truth will out when Fleet Street is no more
And martyrs' blood will cry from shore to shore.
As now today I'm fighting for the Jew
(Since Poles or Finns subsided out of view
Though once the pretext for this war, it's true)
So I have fought for Christians, and my steel
Is always pointed at the tyrant's heel,
Whether from Right or Left he dares to clout
His Maker's image with a butcher's knout.
For Blacks I've done as much, and risked my life,
As since for Jews or Christians in the strife;
When others jumped the liner for Japan
I stayed and faced the music I began.
But you alone with indignation boil

When Hitler dosed the Jews with castor oil—
The world's front window hung with Kosher tripes
And all the Press resounding with their gripes.
Had you been stirred by pity, as by greed,
We might have had a different tale to heed
When half a million Christians had to bleed,
But these were poor and bribed no lawyer's tongue,
Slaughtered by hand, and tortured, heaped, and flung,
To rot like mongrels on a heap of dung,
While you with Herod, and the cash, forsooth
Must blink away the evidence of truth.
But truth will ride and race you to your end,
Propitious enemy and baleful friend!
And as, by night, propelled with frantic strides
A Lion through his forest kingdom rides
Upon the breaking spine of a giraffe
(While all the echoes hold their sides and laugh)
With claws for spurs, and teeth for bridle-chains,
And torn lianas for the flying reins,
And gallops him, with deep, resounding thud
To pitch him headlong in a pool of blood—
So will my verse propel you to your doom,
And give you to the vultures for a tomb!

'Poems for Spain'

No sooner had its sales begun
Than all the reds were on the run
And only halted (sink or swim!)
To hack each other limb from limb—
So, once, at least beneath the sun
Poetic Justice has been done!

Auguries

Prepare for days of pallor,
Forget the waste of breath.
The day has died of valour,
The night will freeze to death.

And if tomorrow wake,
Comrades, no foe to bomb you,
All you had left to take
Will then be taken from you.

Your hunger, sold in books,
Will fetch huge dividends
To salary the cooks
Of other people's friends.

Your poverty, no more
Your own, but in their hands
Another sword of war
To desolate the lands—

What of yourselves you've wrested
From the devouring flames,
Commercialised, invested,
And harnessed to their aims.

The selves you had, so brave
To suffer, help, and share,
Their pity will enslave
To ration with fresh air.

Their pale, commercial pity,
Conscripting thought and art,
That sits in hushed committee
To vivisect the heart.

Glossary

OF WORDS FROM

Arabic, Swahili, Army-English and, elsewhere.

Askari = soldier (white or black).

Bint = a woman (Arabic).

Dhow = lateen-rigged Arab, Persian, or Indian sailing craft.

Skyte-hawk, Kitehawk = euphemisms that rhyme with the soldiers' term for the common camp-scavenging bird: the yellow-billed kite, of the naturalists. It will seize food off a tray as described if the hands of the bearer are both occupied. Many a soldier has lost a good dinner in this way.

Shauri = pronounced to rhyme with cowrie, a dispute, an affair, or discussion.

Safari = a journey or an expedition.

Nat = a tree-spirit, or a forest-gnome.

Four-by-two = a flannel rag used for cleaning the inside of a rifle-barrel with a pull-through.

Talking Bronco = epithet used to describe the author by a leading poet of the Rear.